Assumption School
2310 East 7th Ave.
Hibbing, MN 55746

101 KNOCK-KNOCK JOKES

Make Me Laugh!
101 KNOCK-
guaranteed to make

by Sam Schultz / pictures by Joan Hanson

KNOCK JOKES

even a sourpuss smile

Lerner Publications Company · Minneapolis

Copyright © 1982 by Lerner Publications Company

All rights reserved. International copyright secured. No part of this book may be reproduced in any form whatsoever without permission in writing from the publisher except for the inclusion of brief quotations in an acknowledged review.

Library of Congress Cataloging in Publication Data

Schultz, Sam
  101 knock-knock jokes.

  (Make me laugh)
  Summary: A collection of 101 jokes of the "knock-knock" variety, as: Knock, knock. Who's there? Annie. Annie who? Annie body there?
    1. Knock-knock jokes. 2. Wit and humor, Juvenile. [1. Knock-knock jokes. 2. Jokes. 3. Riddles.] I. Hanson, Joan, ill. II. Title. III. Title: One hundred one knock-knock jokes. IV. Title: One hundred and one knock-knock jokes. V. Series.
  PN6231.K55S3   818'.5402   81-20954
  ISBN 0-8225-0976-8   AACR2

Manufactured in the United States of America

5 6 7 8 9 10 91 90 89

Knock, Knock. Who's there?
Luke. Luke, who?
Luke, I'm standing on my head!

Knock, Knock. Who's there?
Annie. Annie, who?
Annie body home?

Knock, Knock. Who's there?
Boo. Boo, who?
What are you crying about?

Knock, Knock. Who's there?
Ya. Ya, who?
I didn't know you'd be so glad to see me!

Knock, Knock. Who's there?
Ben. Ben, who?
Ben looking all over for you.

Knock, Knock. Who's there?
Abby. Abby, who?
Abby birthday to you.

Knock, Knock. Who's there?
Butternut. Butternut, who?
Butternut let me in. My feet are muddy.

Knock, Knock. Who's there?
Dewey. Dewey, who?
Dewey have to go to school today?

Knock, Knock. Who's there?
Hook. Hook, who?
Hook cares?

Knock, Knock. Who's there?
Isabel. Isabel, who?
Isabel louder than a knock?

Knock, Knock. Who's there?
Boyd. Boyd, who?
Boydo you ask a lot of questions.

Knock, Knock. Who's there?
Candy. Candy, who?
Candy-magine why you'd want to know.

Knock, Knock. Who's there?
Emma. Emma, who?
Emma going to the store. Want to come along?

Knock, Knock. Who's there?
Sam. Sam, who?
Sam times you make me so mad!

Knock, Knock. Who's there?
Alcott. Alcott, who?
Alcott the grass if you'll cut the bushes.

Knock, Knock. Who's there?
Scold. Scold, who?
Scold outside, let me in!

Knock, Knock. Who's there?
Harriet. Harriet, who?
Harriet a whole box of candy.
And now he has a stomachache!

Knock, Knock. Who's there?
Bull. Bull, who?
Bull down the shades. The sun is shining in my eyes.

Knock, Knock. Who's there?
Daniel. Daniel, who?
Daniel so loud. I can hear you.

Knock, Knock. Who's there?
Halibut. Halibut, who?
Halibut letting me borrow a dollar?

Knock, Knock. Who's there?
The force. The force, who?
The force time I knocked, nobody answered!

Knock, Knock.   Who's there?
Juan.   Juan, who?
Juan, two, three, four.

Knock, Knock.   Who's there?
Lena.   Lena, who?
Lena little closer, and I'll whisper in your ear.

Knock, Knock.   Who's there?
Mabel.   Mabel, who?
Mabel I'll tell you, and mabel I won't.

Knock, Knock.   Who's there?
Police.   Police, who?
Police knock a little softer.

Knock, Knock. Who's there?
Henny. Henny, who?
Henny body wanna jump rope?

Knock, Knock. Who's there?
Lion. Lion, who?
Lion only gets me a spanking.

Knock, Knock. Who's there?
Rita. Rita, who?
Rita book and you might learn something.

Knock, Knock. Who's there?
Sawyer. Sawyer, who?
Sawyer lights on, so thought I'd stop by and say hello.

Knock, Knock. Who's there?
Tennis. Tennis, who?
Tennis five plus five.

Knock, Knock. Who's there?
Usher. Usher, who?
Usher would like a piece of chocolate cake!

Knock, Knock. Who's there?
Doris. Doris, who?
Doris open, come on in.

Knock, Knock. Who's there?
Fido. Fido, who?
Fidon't you call me on Saturday?

Knock, Knock. Who's there?
Hugo. Hugo, who?
Hugo to the head of the class.

Knock, Knock. Who's there?
Olive. Olive, who?
Olive right down the street. Where do you live?

Knock, Knock. Who's there?
Harris. Harris, who?
Harris another name for a rabbit.

Knock, Knock. Who's there?
Ice cream. Ice cream, who?
Ice cream, you scream, we all scream for ice cream.

Knock, Knock. Who's there?
Otto. Otto, who?
Otto know if you don't.

Knock, Knock. Who's there?
Paul. Paul, who?
Paul over, buddy, you're driving too fast.

Knock, Knock. Who's there?
Ringo. Ringo, who?
Ringo round the collar.

Knock, Knock. Who's there?
You. You, who?
You-who to you, too!

Knock, Knock. Who's there?
Russell. Russell, who?
Russell up some vittles, pardner. I'm starved!

Knock, Knock. Who's there?
Benny. Benny, who?
Benny for your thoughts.

Knock, Knock. Who's there?
Carmen. Carmen, who?
Carmen over to my house!

Knock, Knock. Who's there?
Gorilla. Gorilla, who?
Gorilla my dreams, I love you.

Knock, Knock. Who's there?
Cecil. Cecil, who?
Cecil have music wherever she goes.

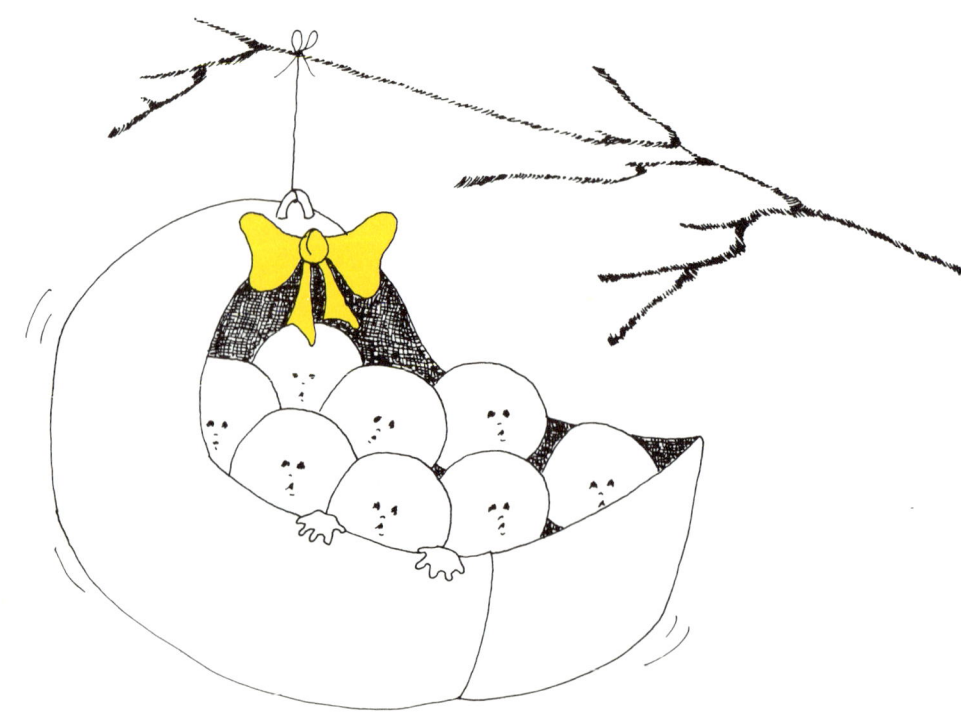

Knock, Knock. Who's there?
Rocky. Rocky, who?
Rocky-bye baby, in the treetop.

Knock, Knock. Who's there?
Hyde. Hyde, who?
Hyde like to tell you, but I can't!

Knock, Knock. Who's there?
Juneau. Juneau, who?
Juneau what time it is?

Knock, Knock. Who's there?
Ron. Ron, who?
Ron and get me a glass of water.

Knock, Knock. Who's there?
Orange. Orange, who?
Orange you glad I came over?

Knock, Knock. Who's there?
Boyer. Boyer, who?
Boyer a sight for sore eyes!

Knock, Knock. Who's there?
Dustin. Dustin, who?
Dustin' and makin' my bed are two things I don't like to do.

Knock, Knock. Who's there?
Jess. Jess, who?
Jess you and me, kid.

Knock, Knock. Who's there?
Fiddlesticks. Fiddlesticks, who?
The fiddlesticks if you don't put rosin on the bow.

Knock, Knock. Who's there?
Holt. Holt, who?
Holt up your hands. I gotcha covered!

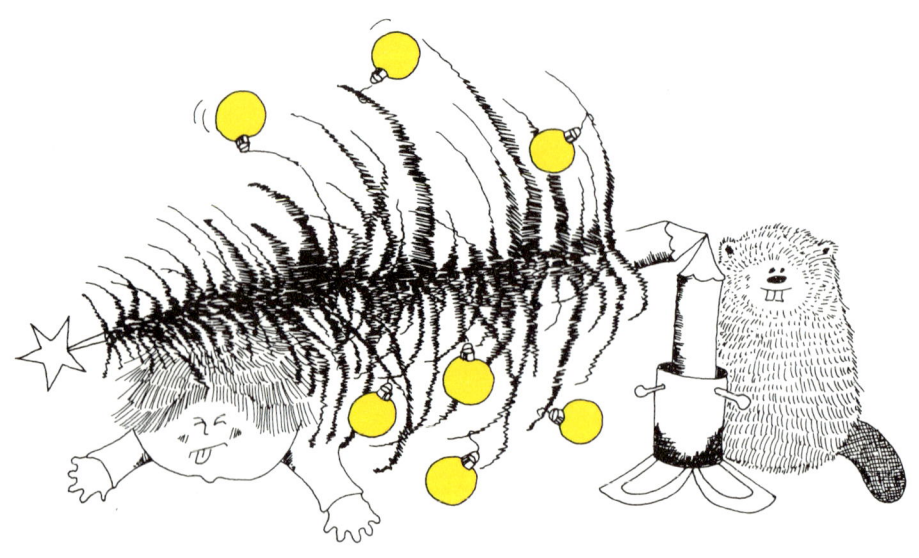

Knock, Knock. Who's there?
Tim. Tim, who?
Tim−ber!!

Knock, Knock. Who's there?
Ivan. Ivan, who?
Ivan to come in!

Knock, Knock. Who's there?
Kent. Kent, who?
Kent you see I'm too busy to talk to you?

Knock, Knock. Who's there?
Max. Max, who?
Max no difference to me!

Knock, Knock. Who's there?
Roxanne. Roxanne, who?
Roxanne stones may break my bones, but names can never hurt me.

Knock, Knock. Who's there?
Justin. Justin, who?
Justin old friend here to see you.

Knock, Knock. Who's there?
Meyer. Meyer, who?
Meyer early. I'm not quite ready yet.

Knock, Knock. Who's there?
Rhoda. Rhoda, who?
Rhoda horse yesterday and fell off.

Knock, Knock. Who's there?
Wendy. Wendy, who?
Wendy you want to come out and play?

Knock, Knock. Who's there?
Heidi. Heidi, who?
Heidi-n here, they'll never find us!

Knock, Knock. Who's there?
Miya. Miya, who?
Miya have a nice pair of shoes!

Knock, Knock. Who's there?
Wade. Wade, who?
Wade and see!

Knock, Knock. Who's there?
Carson. Carson, who?
Carson the highway make lots of smog.

Knock, Knock. Who's there?
Ella. Ella, who?
Ella-mentary school is a grind.

Knock, Knock. Who's there?
Gwen. Gwen, who?
Gwen home, your mother's calling!

Knock, Knock. Who's there?
Hominy. Hominy, who?
Hominy times are you going to ask me?

Knock, Knock. Who's there?
Ida. Ida, who?
Ida wanna tell you.

Knock, Knock. Who's there?
Lemmy. Lemmy, who?
Lemmy a quarter, will you?

Knock, Knock. Who's there?
Otis. Otis, who?
Otis a beautiful day!

Knock, Knock. Who's there?
Stan. Stan, who?
Stan on your own two feet.

Knock, Knock. Who's there?
Yukon. Yukon, who?
Yukon lead a horse to water, but you can't make it drink!

Knock, Knock. Who's there?
Owl. Owl, who?
Owl never tell.

Knock, Knock. Who's there?
Shelby. Shelby, who?
Shelby comin' round the mountain when she comes!

Knock, Knock. Who's there?
Wooden. Wooden, who?
Wooden you like to know?

Knock, Knock. Who's there?
Cashew. Cashew, who?
Gesundheit!

Knock, Knock. Who's there?
Eve. Eve, who?
Eve you want me, just whistle.

Knock, Knock. Who's there?
Francis. Francis, who?
Francis where the Statue of Liberty comes from.

Knock, Knock. Who's there?
Philip. Philip, who?
Philip my glass with another soda.

Knock, Knock. Who's there?
Everett. Everett, who?
Everett all the spinach on your plate?

Knock, Knock.   Who's there?
Who.   Who, who?
What are you, an owl?

Knock, Knock. Who's there?
Burden. Burden, who?
A burden the hand is worth two in the bush.

Knock, Knock. Who's there?
Farm. Farm, who?
Farm-e to know and you to find out.

Knock, Knock. Who's there?
Ellis. Ellis, who?
Ellis the 12th letter of the alphabet.

Knock, Knock. Who's there?
Gopher. Gopher, who?
Gopher a long walk, and don't come back!

Knock, Knock. Who's there?
Rhett. Rhett, who?
Rhett-y or not, here I come!

Knock, Knock. Who's there?
Sarah. Sarah, who?
Sarah doorbell around here? I'm tired of knocking!

Knock, Knock. Who's there?
Nanny. Nanny, who?
Nanny your business!

Knock, Knock. Who's there?
Eaton. Eaton, who?
Eaton between meals is a no-no!

Knock, Knock. Who's there?
Vera. Vera, who?
Vera great team, aren't we?

Knock, Knock.   Who's there?
Doughnut.   Doughnut, who?
Doughnut count your chickens before they're hatched.

Knock, Knock. Who's there?
Pecan. Pecan, who?
Pecan someone your own size!

Knock, Knock. Who's there?
Winnie. Winnie, who?
Winnie you gonna let me in?

Knock, Knock. Who's there?
Sol. Sol, who?
Sol-long, it's been good to see you.

Knock, Knock. Who's there?
Thistle. Thistle, who?
Thistle be the last knock-knock in the book.

Knock, Knock. Who's there?
Les. Les, who?
Les do some more knock-knocks!

ABOUT THE AUTHOR

SAM SCHULTZ began telling jokes to children when his own were very young, and today he likes to think up new jokes while jogging on the beach near his home in Santa Monica, California. Mr. Schultz has been a writer for several advertising agencies, and now he writes scripts for television shows and children's films. He has also written plays, books, and songs. At the University of Southern California, Schultz majored in cinema and creative writing, with an emphasis on humor.

ABOUT THE ARTIST

JOAN HANSON lives with her husband and two sons in Afton, Minnesota. Her distinctive, deliberately whimsical pen-and-ink drawings have illustrated more than 30 children's books. Ms. Hanson is also an accomplished weaver. A graduate of Carleton College, Hanson enjoys tennis, skiing, sailing, reading, traveling, and walking in the woods surrounding her home.

Make Me Laugh!

CAN YOU MATCH THIS?
CAT'S OUT OF THE BAG!
CLOWNING AROUND!
DUMB CLUCKS!
ELEPHANTS NEVER FORGET!
FACE THE MUSIC!
FOSSIL FOLLIES!
GO HOG WILD!
GOING BUGGY!
GRIN AND BEAR IT!
HAIL TO THE CHIEF!
IN THE DOGHOUSE!
KISS A FROG!
LET'S CELEBRATE!
OUT TO LUNCH!
OUT TO PASTURE!
SNAKES ALIVE!
SOMETHING'S FISHY!
SPACE OUT!
STICK OUT YOUR TONGUE!
WHAT A HAM!
WHAT'S YOUR NAME?
WHAT'S YOUR NAME, AGAIN?
101 ANIMAL JOKES
101 FAMILY JOKES
101 KNOCK-KNOCK JOKES
101 MONSTER JOKES
101 SCHOOL JOKES
101 SPORTS JOKES

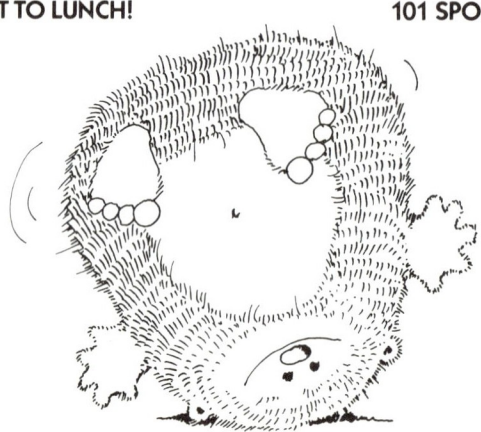